ESSENTIAL SPORTS

basketball

ESSENTIAL SPORTS – BASKETBALL
was produced by

David West 𝕏 **Children's Books**
7 Princeton Court
55 Felsham Road
London SW15 1AZ

First published in Great Britain by Heinemann
Library. Heinemann Library is an imprint of
Pearson Education Limited, a company
incorporated in England and Wales having its
registered office at Edinburgh Gate, Harlow, Essex
CM20 2JE - Registered company number:
00872828

"Heinemann" is a registered trademark of Pearson
Education Limited

Copyright © 2003, 2008 David West Children's
Books

Designed by: Gary Jeffrey
Edited by: James Pickering
Printed in China

ISBN 978 0 431173 85 6 (hardback)
12 11 10 09 08
10 9 8 7 6 5 4 3 2 1
ISBN 978 0 431173 92 4 (paperback)
12 11 10 09 08
10 9 8 7 6 5 4 3 2 1

British Library Cataloguing in Publication Data

Smith, Andy
Basketball. - (Essential Sports)
1. Basketball - Juvenile literature
I. Title
796.3'23

A full catalogue record for this book is available
from the British Library.

Acknowledgements:
We would like to thank the following for
permission to reproduce photographs:

Pages 3 (© NBAE/David Sherman), 4, 19l, 26l (Jamie Squire), 5t (Craig
Jones), 5b (© NBAE/Victor Baldizon), 10l, (© NBAE/Fernando Medina),
7bl, 22-23, 24b (Doug Pensinger), 8l, 13, 17 (Elsa), 10r (© NBAE/Steve
Babineau), 12 (© NBAE/Barry Gossage), 19r (Lisa Blumenfeld), 20l (©
NBAE/Dick Carlson), 20r (Jamie Squire), 21t (Darren McNamara), 11l
(© NBAE/D. Clarke Evans), 11r (Jon Cuban), 14l (© NBAE/Jesse D.
Garrabrant), 14r (© NBAE/Nelson Chenault), 15l & m, 25b (Stephen
Dunn), 15r, 16br (Al Bello), 16t (Ezra Shaw), 18t (Donald Mirelle), 18b
(Norman Trotman), 22t (Brian Bahr), 22b (Scott Cunningham/NBAE),
23, (Matthew Stockman), 24tl (© NBAE/D. Lippitt/Einstein), 25t (©
NBAE/Ron Turenne), 26t (Phil Cole), 26b, (Tom Shaw), 27r (Robert
Mora), 28t (© NBAE/Garrett Ellwood), 28b (Andreas Rentz), 28r
(MLADEN ANTONOV), (29t (Tim de Frusco), 29bl (© NBAE/Brian
Babineau), 30t (Andy Lyons), 21b (NBA Photos), 16bl & bm, 24tr, 29r,
30b - Getty Images. 6tl - The Associated Press Ltd. 6tr & b, 7tl & r - The
Culture Archive. 8r, 12-13 - Corbis Images. 27l - Mini Basketball
England.
*Abbreviations: t-top, m-middle, b-bottom, r-right,
l-left, c-centre.*

Cover photograph: Robert Dozier of The Memphis Tigers puts up a shot
around Brandon Rush of The Kansas Jayhawks by Streeter Lecka
reproduced with permission of Getty Images.

Every effort has been made to contact copyright holders of material
reproduced in this book. Any omissions will be rectified in subsequent
printings if notice is given to the publishers.

*An explanation of difficult words can be
found in the glossary on page 31.*

ESSENTIAL SPORTS

basketball

Andy Smith

REVISED AND UPDATED

Contents

Basketball arguably requires more pace, agility and athleticism than any other sport. Here, Joseph Forte of the North Carolina Tar Heels scores in a college game against the Stanford Cardinal.

The Georgia Dome in Atlanta, USA, packed out for a NCAA (National Collegiate Athletic Association) 'Final Four' game between Indiana and Oklahoma, in March 2002. College basketball provides the bulk of the players who later appear in the NBA.

Introduction

Basketball is probably the fastest-growing sport in the world, although its stronghold is in the country where the modern game was invented at the end of the 19th century – the USA. The beauty of the game is that it is fast and simple, plus almost anyone can play some version of it. Those who are best at playing basketball, however, tend to be powerful, athletic giants. The average professional in the USA's National Basketball Association (NBA), the most important league in the world, is over 1.9 m tall and weighs 106 kg.

Tall, quick, powerful and athletic - Shaquille O'Neal won an NBA Championship with the Miami Heat before moving to the Phoenix Suns in February 2008.

History of the game

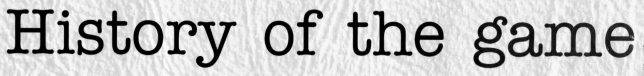

Basketball in its modern form was invented in 1891 by James Naismith, but many years earlier, similar games were being played by civilisations throughout the world.

JAMES NAISMITH

Dr James Naismith, a Canadian, had no knowledge of the early versions of the game when he invented a new sport, to give his Springfield College students something to do indoors on a bitterly cold winter's day. Using baskets nailed to the gym wall and a soccer ball,

Dr James Naismith

he devised a handling game with no physical contact, emphasising skill, not strength. There were 18 students in his class, so the first ever basketball game was nine-a-side. Later, teams of ten were the maximum, only five of whom could be on court at any time.

*It's a simple game.
A backyard, a ball,
a hoop and maybe a
friend to play against
are all you need.*

*Aztecs and Mayans threw the ball
through a stone hoop in the
great ball court in Mexico,
in a game known as
Ollamalitzli.*

LINK WITH THE PAST?

As long ago as the seventh century BC, a game known as Pok-Tapok was played in South and Central America. At each end of a walled open air court, there was a go (basically a stone with a hole throug the middle). The idea was to force the ball through the hole. By the 16th century, 'Ollamalitzli' was being played in Mexico by the Aztecs, using a rubber ball and a stone ring, fixed vertically rather than horizontally. Whoever got the ball through was entitled to claim the clothes of all the spectators!

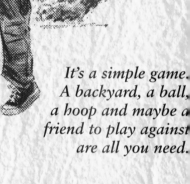

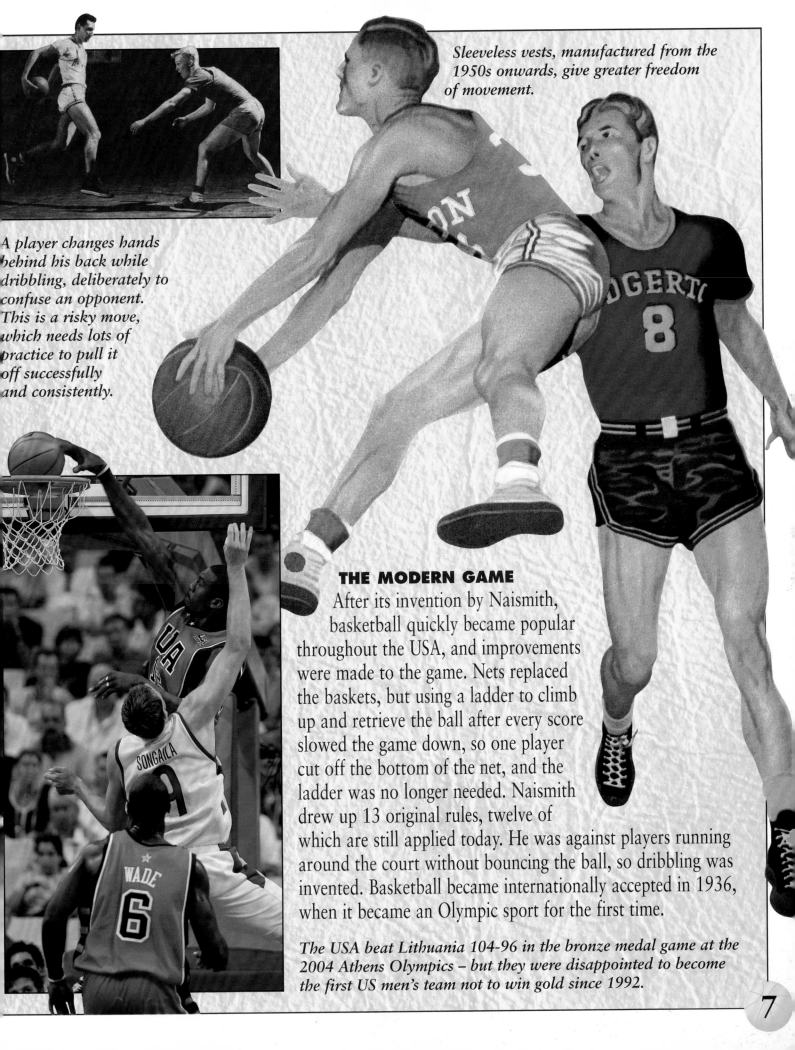

A player changes hands behind his back while dribbling, deliberately to confuse an opponent. This is a risky move, which needs lots of practice to pull it off successfully and consistently.

Sleeveless vests, manufactured from the 1950s onwards, give greater freedom of movement.

THE MODERN GAME

After its invention by Naismith, basketball quickly became popular throughout the USA, and improvements were made to the game. Nets replaced the baskets, but using a ladder to climb up and retrieve the ball after every score slowed the game down, so one player cut off the bottom of the net, and the ladder was no longer needed. Naismith drew up 13 original rules, twelve of which are still applied today. He was against players running around the court without bouncing the ball, so dribbling was invented. Basketball became internationally accepted in 1936, when it became an Olympic sport for the first time.

The USA beat Lithuania 104-96 in the bronze medal game at the 2004 Athens Olympics – but they were disappointed to become the first US men's team not to win gold since 1992.

7

Wear and where

How often do we see basketball kit being worn around town by people who've never been near a basketball court in their life?

THE KIT

Basketball kit isn't just a fashion accessory – it has been developed to give freedom of movement and comfort while also looking good. Players should wear the same coloured shirts which do not clash with the opposition. If numbered, no two players in a team should have the same number. The International Amateur Basketball Federation requires shirts to be numbered between 4 and 15, but the NBA in the USA allows other combinations. So Shaquille O'Neal wore 32 at the Miami Heat and has kept the number with the Phoenix Suns.

Today's players prefer baggy shirts and shorts for maximum mobility. Whatever kit is worn, it's important that it's comfortable and doesn't restrict movement about the court.

THE BALL

The ball is round with an outer casing made of leather, rubber or, more usually these days, a synthetic material. It must bounce correctly – the rebound being between 1.2 m and 1.4 m when dropped from a height of 1.8 m.

Basketball shoes should have rubber soles to give good grip. Decide for yourself whether you need the high-sided version for ankle support. Again, comfort is the key. To prevent blistering, wear two pairs of socks, and shoes a size larger than usual.

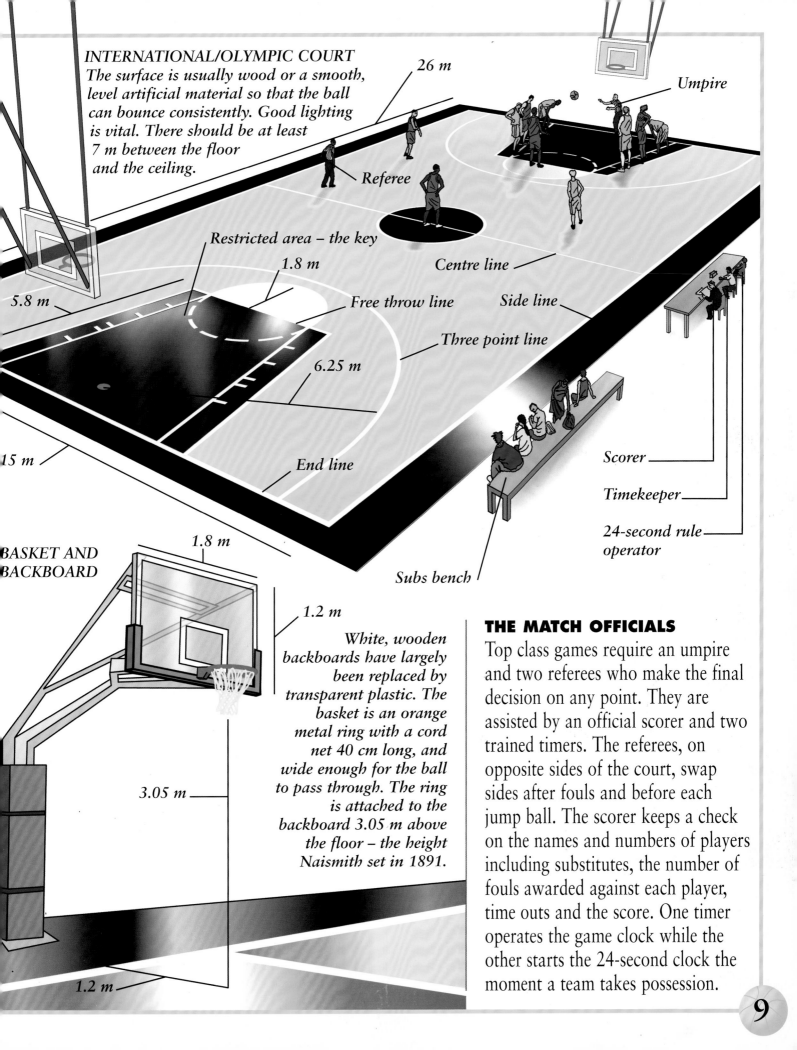

INTERNATIONAL/OLYMPIC COURT
The surface is usually wood or a smooth, level artificial material so that the ball can bounce consistently. Good lighting is vital. There should be at least 7 m between the floor and the ceiling.

26 m

Umpire

Referee

Restricted area – the key

1.8 m

Centre line

5.8 m

Free throw line

Side line

Three point line

6.25 m

15 m

End line

1.8 m

Scorer

Timekeeper

24-second rule operator

Subs bench

BASKET AND BACKBOARD

1.8 m

1.2 m

White, wooden backboards have largely been replaced by transparent plastic. The basket is an orange metal ring with a cord net 40 cm long, and wide enough for the ball to pass through. The ring is attached to the backboard 3.05 m above the floor – the height Naismith set in 1891.

3.05 m

1.2 m

THE MATCH OFFICIALS
Top class games require an umpire and two referees who make the final decision on any point. They are assisted by an official scorer and two trained timers. The referees, on opposite sides of the court, swap sides after fouls and before each jump ball. The scorer keeps a check on the names and numbers of players including substitutes, the number of fouls awarded against each player, time outs and the score. One timer operates the game clock while the other starts the 24-second clock the moment a team takes possession.

What's the point?

The basic idea of the sport is to score more points than the other side, but first your team must take possession.

GAME BASICS

The game is started by a 'jump ball' at the centre. As the referee throws the ball up between two opposing players, the other players must be outside the circle. The jumpers may tap the ball in any direction. The 'jump ball' is also used at the start of overtime and to restart the game after a 'held' or 'dead' ball, when two or more players from opposing sides have their hands on the ball. Once the ball is in play, the team in possession attempts to move into a shooting position.

Two more points for 'Hedo' Turkoglu of the Orlando Magic – the first Turkish born player to play in the NBA.

The opening 'jump ball' in the November 2007 game between the Boston Celtics and the Washington Wizards at Banknorth Garden.

SCORING

A – FIELD GOAL
3 points. When scored from outside the three-point line.
B – FIELD GOAL
2 points. When scored from inside the three-point line.
C – FREE THROW
1 point. Taken from behind the free throw line.

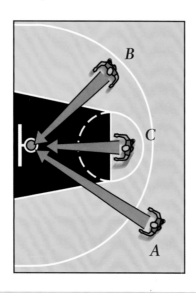

THE PLAYERS

GUARDS
The smallest players on the team. Point guards set up the team's attacks. Shooting guards are the best from long distance.

FORWARDS
Tall, good shooters from either side of the key (see page 9). Quick to rebounds should shots be missed.

CENTRES or POSTS
The tallest players on the team, accurate passers, good shots when close to the basket, jump for rebounds.

MOVING THE BALL

Using both hands to catch, pass or shoot is allowed, but only one hand must be used when dribbling. The ball cannot be hit with a fist or deliberately kicked. Dribbling is the art of bouncing the ball on the move. A dribble ends when both hands touch the ball at once, then the player must pass or shoot. If the ball is received when standing still, the player cannot move, only pivot (turn on one foot) to shoot or pass.

SUBSTITUTES

A coach can substitute any or all of the five players on the court. The substitute makes his way to the scorer who signals when the change can be made. Substitutions can only be made when the ball is 'dead' and the game clock has been stopped. After a violation, the offending team may not make a substitution unless the other side does so.

Substitutes wait on the sidelines until the scorer and officials signal them on to the court.

Awareness! Dribbling at speed with head up – the Toronto Rangers' T. J. Ford against the San Antonio Spurs in February 2007.

POSITIONS

Teams use different formations, depending on the state of the game and the tactics to be used against the opposition. A 2–1–2 formation is usually a defensive formation. 1–2–2 is a standard formation.

2–1–2 FORMATION

Centre

Forward

Forward

Guard

Centre

Guard

Guard

Forward

Forward

Centre

1–2–2 LINE UP

Time is of the essence

Apart from four quarters of ten minutes each, (twelve in the pro game), basketball has time limits set for various actions. It makes the game quick and exciting.

Restarting after a basket. The defending team throws the ball in from behind the endline.

TIME LIMITS RULES

These vary according to the standard of the game. In the professional game the 30-second rule is reduced to 24 seconds.

30 *Having gained possession, the team has 30 seconds in which to shoot at the basket.*

10 *If a team gains possession in its own half, it has ten seconds to move the ball into its opponents' half.*

5 *On a throw-in or a free throw, a player must put the ball in play within five seconds. A closely-marked player must also release the ball within five seconds.*

3 *A player must not stay in the opposition's restricted area for more than three seconds, except when the ball is in the air on a try for goal or when it rebounds from the backboard.*

FOULS

Fouls in basketball are either 'personal' or 'technical'. Personal fouls are committed against an opponent, and include blocking, holding, pushing, charging and tripping. Technical fouls can be committed by players, coaches or substitutes, and include anything which is against the spirit of the game, such as unsporting behaviour or bad language. Personal fouls come in various forms, for example normal, intentional or disqualifying, plus fouls on a player about to shoot. All carry different penalties.

The personal space, or body zone, of a player in possession of the ball includes the floor and an imaginary cylinder around the body. If another player makes contact within this zone, it is a personal foul.

Personal foul by Tim Duncan of the San Antonio Spurs on guard Raja Bell of the Phoenix Suns.

PENALTIES

For a technical foul, two free throws are awarded against the offending team, and for accidental contact with an opponent (normal personal foul), a throw from the sideline is awarded. An intentional foul incurs two free throws. Striking an opponent (disqualifying foul) results in the offender being replaced. A foul on a player in the act of shooting could result in up to three free throws.

A time-out may be called when the ball is dead and the clock stopped.

TIME-OUT

Two time-outs are allowed per team per half, plus one each in periods of overtime. The ball must be 'dead' and the clock stopped at the moment the time-out is called, or after a team's opponents have scored a field goal. A time-out lasts one minute. In the NBA, seven time-outs are allowed per game plus one 20-second time-out.

TECH TIPS - TAKING A FREE THROW

With no opponents allowed to challenge, a free shot should mean a certain point.

Knees slightly bent, feet apart, stand behind, not on, the free throw line.

Shoot with either hand, the ball in the finger pads not the palm. Keep your eyes on the target.

Straighten legs and release the ball on its way and follow through. Practice should ensure a high success rate.

Close control

When in possession, every player must feel comfortable on the ball, which means that they must have the skills to be in control of the ball at all times.

Even the experts aren't always perfect – Jamaal Thomas of the Alberquerque Thunderbirds just keeps control against the Arkansas RimRockers.

Paul Pierce of the Boston Celtics ready to pivot and pass against the Philadelphia 76ers.

DRIBBLING

Dribbling – moving around the court while bouncing the ball with one hand – is the main alternative to passing the ball. Players should practise until they are able to dribble without always looking at the ball, bounce the ball with either hand and be able to change direction to escape opponents. For beginners, start practising bouncing the ball while standing still, then move around when more confident.

TECH TIPS – DRIBBLING TECHNIQUES

PROTECTED DRIBBLE
It is the opponent's job to take the ball from you. Learn how to protect the ball.
1 Bounce the ball on your side away from the defender, position yourself between the ball and your opponent.
2 Bar the way to the ball with your arm.

SPEED DRIBBLE
To shake off a defender, dribble at speed. Push the ball further ahead when running, keep your head up to watch the ball and for any challenges. Be ready to change back to a protected dribble when an opponent comes in.

TECH TIPS – CHANGING HANDS

When dribbling, you will have to change hands to keep the ball away from a defender.

1

CROSS OVER
Change the ball over with one bounce in front of you. You can only touch the ball with one hand at a time when dribbling.

BETWEEN THE LEGS
Practice can make this move perfect – it's an impressive technique.
1 To pass from right to left hand, bounce the ball under the extended left leg.
2 Collect in the left hand, continue dribbling.

2

BEHIND THE BACK
Another advanced technique that needs plenty of practice. Move slightly ahead of the ball, twist your fingers as it's passed behind your back to bounce up into the other hand.

FOOTWORK

A dribble comes to an end when the player puts both hands on the ball. Then the player may pivot on one foot to pass or shoot, or take advantage of the two step rule, one step with either foot, before releasing. Players use two methods to stop when finishing a dribble – the stride stop and the jump stop.

The stride stop – Greco caught the ball with both feet off the ground, used one pace to stop, takes another step to pass.

Michelle Greco of UCLA after a jump stop, lands with both feet on the floor, ready to bounce pass.

SKILL DRILL – ONE-ON-ONE

All practice is beneficial but playing a simple game of one-on-one with a team mate helps to improve both attacking and defensive skills. Each player takes turns to attack from outside the key, while the other defends. As soon as a basket is scored, or a rebound is collected by the defender, the roles are reversed.

Passing

Passing is the safest method of keeping possession. It is also a quicker way of moving the ball down court than by dribbling. Basketball is a team passing game.

The chest pass is the basic pass used in the game – quick and simple.

BASIC PASSING SKILLS

Passing the ball is not simply offloading it on to another player. The receiver must take the ball when and where he wants it. Accuracy is the key to good passing, giving the receiver the option to dribble, pass or shoot. Ideally, passes should be disguised. Give no hint of the intended receiver by looking in their direction or taking too long over the pass. The pass should be short and direct.

OVERHEAD PASS
The important thing is to find your team mate.
1 Ball in both hands as for a chest pass
2 Step in the direction of the pass, push the ball in the air, over the opponent and into the hands of the receiver.

TECH TIPS – OTHER WAYS OF PASSING

HAND OFF PASS
One player tries to slip the ball to a team mate. Here an opposing player attempts to steal the ball.

BOUNCE PASS
Used against taller opponents or a player with arms up, blocking other routes to a team mate. Using one or two hands in a low position, bounce the ball across to the receiver, eluding the opponent. Being a slower pass, it is easier to intercept, so be careful!

JAVELIN PASS
A one-handed overhead pass designed for speed and distance to set up fast breaks, often out of defence to a team mate in shooting range.

RECEIVING THE BALL

There is nothing more frustrating than wasting a good pass. To reduce the risk of dropping and losing the ball from a pass, keep your eyes on the ball at all times. Keep moving around the court so that the passer can find you 'open' (unmarked). Indicate where you want the ball to go with your right or left hand. Decide what you are going to do with it.

Receive the pass with both hands, with your fingers around the ball protected in the triple threat position, knees bent, elbows spread, ball under chin. Decide quickly whether to pass, dribble or shoot.

TECH TIPS - BREAKING FREE

Breaking free is the art of finding space away from your opponent, leaving you open to receive a pass. Several movements may be required.

With the passing route closed by your opponent, look for space inside and move towards the basket.

With your opponent moving behind you to cover, signal to the passer to pass into your original position.

Use the advantage of the space you've created to receive the pass.

SKILL DRILL - PASSING PRACTICE

You don't need the rest of the team to practise your passing skills – a ball, a wall and an open space will do.

Make chest passes over a metre or two at the wall. Take the ball on the bounce and repeat several times. Then vary it. Throw the chest pass, take the rebound and play the bounce pass. Repeat, aiming for 100 per cent accuracy against a mark on the wall. Add in the overhead and the javelin pass. This is a good pre-game practice drill.

Shooting

The whole point of the game is to score more points than your opponents – so shooting is vital.

GETTING ON TARGET

Being balanced, under control and concentrating on the basket are essential for being on target. Long range shots are spectacular when successful, but the closer to the basket you are, the more chance you have of scoring points. There are various types of shots that all players, whatever position, should practise.

Matt Barnes of UCLA leaps up to dunk a rebound against the Hawaii Rainbow Warriors

TECH TIPS – LAY UP SHOT

An attacker receives the ball, and with no defender in front of the basket, dribbles in to jump and shoot the ball off the backboard and into the basket.

Coming in from the left side of the basket, jump and use the left hand for the shot. Breaking in from the right, use the right hand. Remember that after dribbling, only two steps are allowed, so the second should be the take off into the jump.

Use the backboard – place the ball into the square above the ring and it will drop through. Too hard, and it will bounce away.

When shooting, one hand should be behind and slightly under the ball, wrist cocked back, with the supporting hand at the side

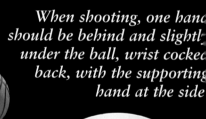

Marcus Tony of the Seton Hall Pirates using the set shot technique for a free throw (see page 13). Some players use both hands to achieve a similar result

TECH TIPS – JUMP SHOT

This shot uses a similar technique to the set shot for free throws. When in this position, keep calm and concentrate on the basket.

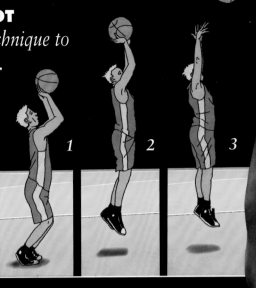

1 Knees bent, eyes on the target, bring the ball above your head. 2 Straighten the legs to jump upwards, not forwards, still concentrating. 3 Release the ball at the top of the jump, follow through with a flick of the wrists.

A hook shot is a version of the lay up shot. But instead of coming from a distance, the attacker is closer, faces away from the basket, pivots and jumps.

CLOSE IN SHOTS

One of the most effective shots from close range is the dunk, but the attacker needs to be very tall or a good jumper – the basket is 3 m off the floor! The player jumps high, the ball in one hand above the basket and dunks, or stuffs, the ball down through the ring. When facing away from the basket, try the hook shot.

Devean George, of the 2001–02 NBA champions the Los Angeles Lakers, is up for a slam dunk against the San Antonio Spurs.

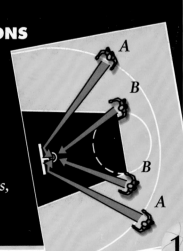

SKILL DRILL – SHOOTING STATIONS

Practise shooting by picking out four spots around the basket, one and two steps away.

Using the set shot or jump shot technique, shoot for the basket from various points. Then from the same points, but with your back to the target, practise the hook shot.

19

Michael Joiner of the Sioux Falls Skyforce drives into Rio Grande Valley defender Gabe Muoneke.

Offence

The aim of every attacking team is to complete the move with a shot on target. First though, they have to get within range.

TEAMWORK

Individuals have responsibility within the team. A player must always think about how to benefit the team – shoot, dribble, pass or move – while always trying to face forwards to the basket, pass forwards, move ahead of team mates and find space. Always try to set up a scoring chance, outwit the defence and be aware of any rebound possibilities.

D.J. Augustin of the Texas Longhorns breaks away from the Kansas Jayhawks at Allen Fieldhouse, Kansas.

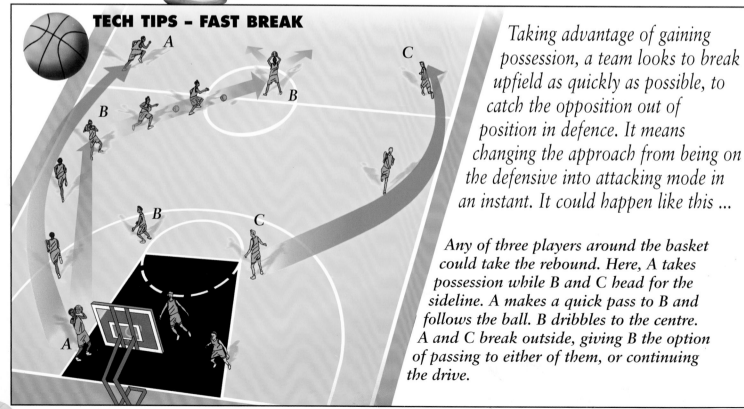

TECH TIPS – FAST BREAK

Taking advantage of gaining possession, a team looks to break upfield as quickly as possible, to catch the opposition out of position in defence. It means changing the approach from being on the defensive into attacking mode in an instant. It could happen like this ...

Any of three players around the basket could take the rebound. Here, A takes possession while B and C head for the sideline. A makes a quick pass to B and follows the ball. B dribbles to the centre. A and C break outside, giving B the option of passing to either of them, or continuing the drive.

ATTACKING FROM REBOUNDS

Even the best teams can only turn about 45 per cent of their chances into points. Teamwork is not only crucial to set up shots in the first place, but also to have players in position to take the rebounds for a chance of a second shot. Attackers should watch the initial shot for a rebound, jump up with both arms extended and attempt another basket instantly. If a two-handed catch is impossible, the ball should be tipped back towards the basket to give another attacker a chance.

The Skyforce's Michael Joiner and Nick Lewis of the Iowa Energy (in white) compete for a rebound at the Wells Fargo Arena, Des Moines, Iowa.

TECH TIPS – SCREEN PLAY

Screen play is an attacking tactic used against a one-on-one defence.

The player in possession moves with her marker towards a team mate, who stands blocking the line the defender must use to stay with the attacker. The attacker can now draw another marker, freeing up another team mate, or head for the basket. For the player who has blocked the defender, the move is known as a 'pick and roll' as he turns and heads for the basket.

ATTACKING A ZONE DEFENCE

Zone defence (see page 25) was outlawed by the NBA until 2001. Today, teams shoot more often from long range. It makes for a more varied game.

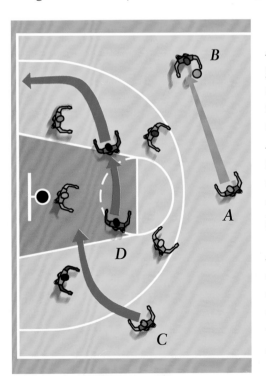

Attacking player A passes the ball to attacking player B, who shoots from outside the zone. Attackers C and D move to draw defenders away. C and A will be poised for the rebound.

Alternatively, the attacking side overloads one side to draw the defence, while quick passing exploits the gaps on the other side.

Individual defence

When the opposition has the ball, the defence's job is to prevent them having a shot at the basket, by stealing the ball or forcing them to run out of time in possession.

PRESSURISING THE OPPOSITION

Defence is best done as a team, but individual defence is frequently called upon. When marking the ball carrier, stand between the opponent and the basket. When marking an attacker without the ball, move into a position so that you can watch the opponent and the ball. Analyse your opponent's strengths and weaknesses. Are they able to use both hands to pass? Can they dribble with both hands? Are they weak in the air?

No. 5, Demetrius Porter of Fresno State, makes it difficult for Mike Kelley to find a Wisconsin team mate.

TECH TIPS - DEFENDING OUT OF SHOOTING RANGE

Use the basic stance, but with hands low, ready to steal the ball given a chance. If the player attempts to dribble past, keep one hand as close to the ball as possible, to snatch it away. If the opponent tries to pass, be ready with your hands up.

22

Expert defence by the Utah Jazz as Juwan Howard's shot for the Houston Rockets is blocked in the 2007 play-off game.

Steve Blake of the University of Maryland spreads himself in defensive mode, as Michael Joseph of the Citadel nears the basket.

DEFENDING CLOSE TO THE BASKET

Take up a position between the opponent and the basket, using hands and arms to cover an attempted pass or shot. The defensive stance should be close enough to the attacker to discourage a shot, but contact cannot be made. Flex the knees, keep the head up, stand feet apart with one foot slightly in front of the other to turn quickly if required.

TECH TIPS – MOVING WITH YOUR OPPONENT

In one-on-one defence, keep your eyes on the ball all the time. Interceptions are vital.

1 Maintain the defensive stance, cover every move of the opponent by moving sideways, forwards or backwards.

2 Stay balanced. If the attacker attempts to dribble past, drop one foot back and move across to close down the space.

3 If the defender moves backwards to pass, take a step forwards, hands ready to intercept the ball.

Team defence

Individual defensive skills are used within the team's tactics to prevent the opposition scoring.

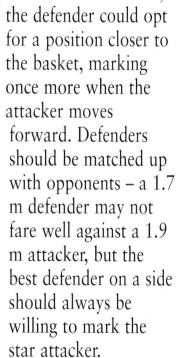

San Francisco Dons' James Cobb attempts to dribble past his marker Andre Miller.

ONE-ON-ONE MARKING

This is the simplest defensive strategy to employ. Each defender is given an opponent to mark around the court. Defenders need to concentrate on their opponent's position as well as the ball. If the attacking player hangs back in his own half, the defender could opt for a position closer to the basket, marking once more when the attacker moves forward. Defenders should be matched up with opponents – a 1.7 m defender may not fare well against a 1.9 m attacker, but the best defender on a side should always be willing to mark the star attacker.

The Dallas Mavericks' Brandon Bass (32) and DeSagana Diop stretch to block an attempt by the Detroit Pistons' guard Rodney Stuckey.

One-on-one marking is already in evidence at the jump off in a women's professional league game between New York Liberty and Houston Comets.

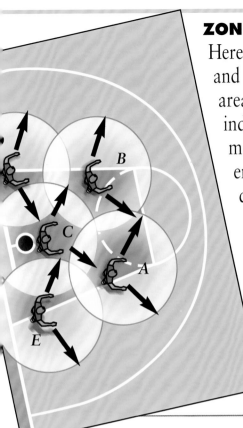

ZONE DEFENCE

Here, all five defenders work as a team and concentrate on the ball, covering areas of the court rather than individual players. Protecting the key makes it difficult to move in close enough to shoot. Until recently, zone defence was banned in the NBA – now we see more long range shots.

A typical zone defence formation – 2–1–2 with the two smaller players, guards A and B, at the front. The tallest player – C – is positioned in the middle. Most shots should come in from a distance against this formation.

DEFENDING REBOUNDS

Every time a shot is missed, the defending side has a chance to take possession and turn defence into attack. To be successful, the defenders must block out the five attackers.

A brilliant steal by Chris Bosh of the Toronto Raptors.

Quick thinking by Mario Bennett of Arizona State makes him first to the rebound against UCLA.

TECH TIPS – BLOCKING OUT

This is an essential technique for regaining possession on the rebound.

1 Take a position between the attacker and the basket.
2 Pivot, turning your back on your opponent, making a barrier between the attacker and the possible rebound ball.
3 Eyes on the ball, leap as high as possible to catch the ball out of reach of your opponent.

Basketball variations

D reams of playing in the NBA cannot come true for everyone, but you can still enjoy the game at whatever level you play.

WHEELCHAIR BASKETBALL

For wheelchair basketball competitors, the rules are slightly adapted, but the same court and the same ball are used. The game can be played by anyone, as long as they are able to propel their own wheelchair. In wheelchair basketball, a jump ball is only used at the start of each half. When the ball goes out of play, the teams alternate in taking throw-ins from the sidelines. When dribbling in wheelchair basketball, a player is allowed to rest the ball on the lap while pushing the chair. Up to two pushes must be followed by one or more bounces. Instead of using a three-second rule, five seconds are allowed before a player must shoot or pass.

Britain's Simon Munn is blocked by Brad Ness of Australia in the Athens 2004 Paralympic Games semi-final.

Lisa Chaffey of Australia and Stephanie Wheeler of the USA in a tussle during the final of the 2004 Paralympic Games in Athens.

MINI BASKETBALL

Mini basketball is for nine- to twelve-year-olds. The ring is 2.6 m above the court, and the ball is smaller than the standard ball. The game is divided into four quarters of ten minutes each. Each player must play at least one quarter, but no player can play in all the first three quarters. There is no 30-second rule when an attacking team must take a shot at the basket, no time-outs, substitutions (except between quarters) or bonus free throws, when a player is fouled in the act of scoring.

Mini basketball at the Italian North Jamboree competition in 1999

SLAMBALL! Coming to a TV screen near you soon!

SLAMBALL

Slamball was created for American television by Mason Gordon in 2002. Combining elements of basketball, football, hockey and gymnastics, the game is played with four trampolines set into the floor around each basket. It is claimed that the competitors perform athletic feats 'never seen before in professional sports'. Each team has a squad of eight players, only four of which may be on court during a game. Slamball's first foreign tournament was in Italy in 2007.

The world of basketball

Basketball became a truly international sport when it gained entry to the Olympics for the first time in 1936 at Berlin.

INTERNATIONAL COMPETITIONS

Basketball is one of the world's foremost spectator sports. The first European Championship was held in 1935 when Latvia were the winners, while the first ever World Championship was won by Argentina in 1950. The women's World Championship was first staged in 1953. In Britain the highlight of the season is the play-off and finals weekend in Sheffield in April. The NBA in the USA is the world's premier league, with top players from all over the world, alongside Americans.

In the 2006 FIBA World Championship semi-final in Japan, Greece beat the USA but lost in the final to Spain.

THE OLYMPICS

Basketball players at the Olympics were strictly amateur until 1992. Three years earlier, the International Federation had abolished the distinction between amateur and professional, allowing professionals from the NBA to compete in the Olympics for the first time. It was no surprise when the 'Dream Team', featuring Michael Jordan, Magic Johnson and Larry Bird won gold!

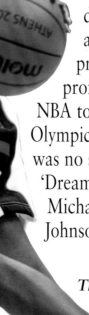

Argentina beat Italy 84-69 in the 2004 men's Olympic Final in Athens.

The USA women's team took the gold in the 2004 Olympics with a 74-63 victory over Australia.

STARS OF THE SPORT

The famous Harlem Globetrotters were founded in 1927 as a team of professional players touring the USA, playing exhibition matches and giving demonstrations. Soon they were travelling further afield with their amusing and skilful routines, delighting spectators the world over, one of their stars being the extrovert Meadowlark Lemon. The NBA, with increased global TV coverage has seen its stars attain world profiles – Bird, Johnson and Jordan from the first 'Dream Team', followed by the likes of Shaquille O'Neal and Allen Iverson. The Women's NBA in the USA was founded in 1997. The Phoenix Mercury won the 2007 championship beating defending champions Detroit Shock in the finals.

The Harlem Globetrotters entertain spectators all over the world with their unique, acrobatic brand of basketball.

Michael Jordan in the colours of the Chicago Bulls. Ten times the NBA's leading scorer, he emerged from retirement in 2001, to play for the Washington Wizards.

Dirk Nowittzki of the Dallas Mavericks, one of the outstanding talents in the modern game, on target again against the Boston Celtics at Banknorth Garden.

Health and fitness

An injured player is no use to the team. Make sure that you are always available for selection by following a simple guide to keeping in good shape, as well as practising basketball skills.

Jason Williams of the USA warms up before the 1999 Nike Hoop summit game, with a few groin and inner thigh stretching exercises.

WARMING UP AND DOWN

Going on to a court 'cold' could mean the difference between losing early points and being in control from the start. A few minutes' skipping or light running strengthens legs and aids footwork. Swinging each arm up and round warms up arms and shoulders. To avoid hamstring injuries, sit on the floor, legs together, out in front. Slide your hands down your thighs, stretching as far as possible towards your ankles. Hold for five seconds. Repeat five times. To stretch your thighs, stand against a wall, back straight, bend one knee to raise the foot behind you. Hold for five seconds. Repeat five times for each leg. Use similar exercises after games to warm down.

DEHYDRATION

Playing at full pace, with maximum effort, can result in dehydration. To guard against it, sip small quantities of liquid before, during and after the game.

Everybody has their own idea of what suits them best. Isotonic drinks are useful to prevent dehydration when playing, practising or training. If you don't like them, stick to good old water! But remember, too much liquid on board is just as bad as too little, and very uncomfortable.

The hamstring stretch is a useful warm up exercise. Take it easy at first, but aim to lengthen your stretch down to your ankles each time. You can't play with an injured hamstring.

Warming down ensures that you are fit to play or practise the next day. Muscles that have become taut during the game should be gradually relaxed. Otherwise they'll feel tight and sore.

Glossary

BACKBOARD the board at the back of the basket

BACK COURT the half of the court a team is defending

BASKET the name for the target, and also a score

DEHYDRATION excessive loss of liquid from the body

DRIBBLE moving with the ball while bouncing it with one hand

DUNK OR STUFF when a player leaps up and stuffs the ball through the hoop

FAST BREAK moving the ball quickly from defence to attack

FREE THROW an unopposed penalty throw at the basket

FRONT COURT the half of the court the opponents are defending

HAMSTRING tendon at the back of the knee, easily but painfully pulled when cold

KEY the keyhole-shaped area at the end of each court

NBA National Basketball Association, the top league in the world

ONE-ON-ONE defensive method when one player marks another

SCREEN PLAY an attacking tactic used against a zone defence

TRAVELLING illegal dribbling through failing to bounce the ball properly

ZONE DEFENCE method in which defensive players mark an area of the court

Further information

National Basketball Association (NBA)
Women's National Basketball Association (WNBA)
Olympic Tower,
645 5th Ave,
New York, NY 10022
USA
http://www.nba.com
http://www.wnba.com

England Basketball
PO Box 3971,
Sheffield,
S9 9AZ
http://www.englandbasketball.com

Basketball Association of Wales
http://www.basketballwales.com

Scottish Basketball Association
http://www.basketball-scotland.com

National Basketball League (Australia)
PO Box 7141,
Alexandria,
NSW, 2015
www.nbl.com.au

Great Britain Wheelchair Basketball Association
Loughborough Park,
Oakwood Drive,
Loughborough,
Leicestershire,
LE11 3NG
http://www.gbwba.org.uk

Index